WITHDRAWN

101 GIFTS AND NOVELTIES CHILDREN CAN MAKE

ALL YEAR ROUND

BY BECKY SHAPIRO

STERLING PUBLISHING CO., Inc.

MAYFLOWER • London

Contents

© Copyright 1958
by Sterling Publishing Co., Inc.
419 Fourth Ave., New York 16, N. Y.
Manufactured in the United States of America
Library of Congress Catalog Card No.: 58-12541

Third Printing, April, 1960

61319

Foreword

The ideas in this book are original and have been play-room-tested. They have been created for the purpose of bringing pleasure to and exciting the imagination of children, anywhere, any time. The objects are easy to make from material that is usually already within reach. By following the simple directions you will be proud of the results.

For best results, be sure that you retain in your household such ordinary useful objects as empty milk cartons, cereal boxes, tissue boxes, tissue paper rolls, tooth paste boxes, paper bags, plastic vegetable bags and cellophane tape dispensers. Besides these, it would be well to have on hand at all times colored cellophane tape as well as plain cellophane tape; colored construction paper and crepe paper; library paste or rubber cement; wax; ribbon and colored strings; woolen yarn of various colors; paper muffin cups, paper lace doilies, soda straws; poster paints and enamel; and nail polish.

The projects in this book will be easier to make if you use the materials recommended, but in some cases, you will be able to substitute.

I. Gifts for Any Time

CORK ANIMAL

An unusual-looking animal that you might like to give someone can be made from an ordinary cork. Run carpet tack legs into the cork as shown, then make the face with thumbtacks. Whittle the end of a small wooden matchstick into a point and stick it into the large end of the cork to form the animal's tail.

It can be used as a ring holder (the tail) or as a pincushion (the body) or can just be decorative.

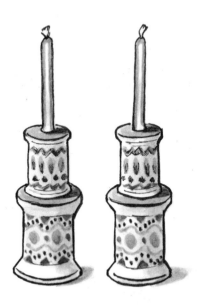

CANDLEHOLDERS

A pair of gift candleholders can be made from some empty wooden spools. Wash the spools to remove the paper labels and, when they are dry, glue them together, placing the bigger spools at the bottom. Paint and decorate the candleholders with water colors. Now soften the ends of small party candles and fit them into the holders, as shown in the above sketch.

HANGING VASE

Any member of your family or a friend would be happy to receive this dainty hanging vase. To make it, first decorate half of an eggshell with pale water-color stripes. Then fasten a ribbon handle securely to the sides with cellophane tape. Pour water into the shell (it won't leak) and fill it with ivy or an arrangement of tiny flowers and leaves.

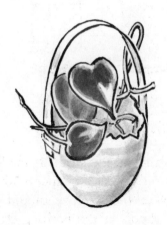

MAIL HOLDER

This handy holder for letters that come in every day is made from a two-piece cardboard box. Pull the top end of the smaller part of the box down flat, as shown. Now cut the lid of the box about 4 inches up from the bottom. Fit this over the other part of the box and tape it in back with cellophane tape.

This mail holder can be fastened to the wall in the kitchen or to some other convenient place with a thumbtack.

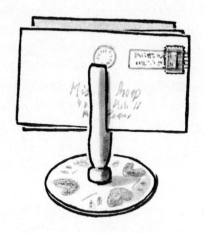

LETTER HOLDER

Here's another handy letter holder. To make it, cut a circle from heavy cardboard or use the top of a round cardboard cheese box. Push a thumbtack up through the center of the circle, then press the top of a wooden clothespin down on the thumbtack end. Decorate the base with crayon designs.

NAME HANDKERCHIEF

Anyone would be happy to receive a gift handkerchief with his (or her) name on it. All you do is write out the name in pencil, then with colored embroidery thread follow the pencil line carefully with tiny stitches. Something very special would be a handkerchief with an embroidered message, such as "Happy Birthday, Connie" or "Good Luck, Jimmy."

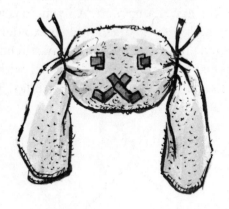

WASHCLOTH DOG

A washcloth and a cake of soap fashioned into the shape of a dog's head makes a suitable gift for someone who is going away to camp. Place the soap in the center of the cloth, then wrap the cloth around it. Form the floppy ears by gathering up the cloth and tying it tightly with ribbon. Make the eyes, nose and mouth with pieces of colored tape.

NATURE BOY

This mantel decoration is made from a cardboard bathroom tissue tube. Cover the top half of the tube with plain white paper and the bottom half with colored paper. From the colored paper also cut the eyes, nose and mouth. Paste them down, then wind a satin ribbon at the neck and fasten it in place with a straight pin. Fill the center with evergreen or other greenery that doesn't require water.

ALMOND NECKLACE

This unusual necklace is easy to make. First fill a cup with water, then soak the pointed ends of five almonds in the water for about a minute each. Now use a large needle to run a string through each nut. Tie the string at the top of each almond. When the almonds are dry, paint faces on them with water colors.

POUCH BAG

Make a handy little pouch bag from an unused colored paper baking cup. With a large embroidery needle run a length of yarn about 20 inches long very carefully through the folds of the paper cup about ¼ of an inch from the top. When you are halfway around the cup leave a loop of yarn, then continue on. When you get back to the starting point, form another loop by knotting the yarn ends together. The two loops will act as purse strings as you open the bag's mouth. You and all your friends will want to own pouch bags.

DESK HANDYMAN

An interesting doll that will hold rubber bands or metal paper clips is made by cutting two one-inch-wide rings from a cardboard roll. With a heavy needle make holes in the rings. Now fasten the rings together (as in the drawing) with a toothpick. Use toothpicks for arms and legs, then stick the legs into an eraser or clay base so it will stand up firmly.

HAWAIIAN LEI

Cut tissue paper into strips 3 inches wide by 6 inches long. Paint colored borders on some of the strips. Then fold the paper in half lengthwise and make slits along the edges leaving a half-inch band near the center fold. Unfold the strips and, with a needle, run string through the center of each paper, gathering the strips together to form the loose necklace which the Hawaiians call a "lei."

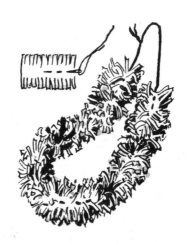

FISH DISH

From paper plates you can make tropical fish dishes that may be displayed on a table, hung on the wall or presented to your friends. Letting the flat center form the body of the fish, draw the outline of the mouth, fins and tail on the rim of the plate. After you have cut out the fish, color it with crayons. Select bright colors that will show up well.

POTTED PLANT

To make this tiny artificial plant, start by cutting a soda straw into two 3-inch lengths. Slit the straws down the center, then use cellophane tape to fasten the ends of the branches to the backs of party-cake flowers. Place the straws in the center of a wooden spool and cover the spool with silver paper. The result should look like the drawing.

PAPER PETUNIAS

Flatten two milk-bottle hoods slightly by pulling out the sides. Then color the centers with crayon. Push the end of a pipe cleaner stem through a hole in the center of each and press the ends down. Cut leaves from construction paper. Punch a hole at one end of each leaf and run the stems through them.

BOTTLE GRANDMA

Use an empty medicine bottle to make this Grandma doll. To make the head, crumple tissue paper into a ball, cover it with more tissue paper and twist the ends into a point. Draw the facial features with ink, paste cotton "hair" in place and then put the pointed end into the bottle. The ribbon collar is pasted together in the back.

The skirt and shawl can be made from scraps of fabric. The skirt is gathered at the waist with a rubber band. A pin holds the shawl in place.

This makes a nice gift for Grandma, which she can keep at her house to let you play with.

TIN-TOP TINKLER

This tinkler, when hung out of doors, will make a pleasant sound whenever the wind blows. To make it, punch a hole near the edge of three tin can tops, then punch a hole in the center of a fourth top and three more holes around this, as shown in the top part of the drawing. Connect the tops with string. Then run a knotted string through the center hole of the top tin for hanging. Poster paint mixed with soap powder may be used to put decorative designs on the tin tops, though enamel would be more permanent.

TOY TRAY

This toy tray, which can be used to hold grapes, nuts or raisins, will make a nice gift for a friend. Punch a hole through the center of a metal jar lid. Then run a tack through the hole and into a cork. To make the tray especially attractive, paint it with any enamel you have around the house. Mom or Dad will probably be glad to help with the painting.

FLOWER TRAY

The lid of a waxed cardboard container, the kind that cottage cheese comes in, is used to make this attractive flower tray. Pull the rim up at opposite sides. Push holes through the sides, run pipe cleaners through them and make the handle as shown. Now decorate the tray with colorful ribbon bows. Put some water in the tray and a few flowers.

WIRE ANIMALS

Animals that look almost like real works of modern art can be made from wire that you find around the house or from rubber-covered wire that can be purchased in the dime store. Cut the wire into about 15-inch lengths, then from this sketch or any model form the animal shape by twisting and coiling the wires. Use as many pieces of wire as you find necessary.

HAIRPIN FIGURES

You will find small wire hairpins easy to bend and fun to twist into different shapes. Make the figure in the illustration, first forming the arms. Then make the head by twisting another hairpin securely around the arms. Bend a third hairpin into a "running-legs" position and slip it through the arm loop. Hang the figure on a nail on the wall.

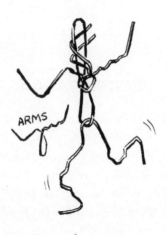

CHUCK WAGON

Here is a nice party favor that you can make. Cut a piece of plain white paper to measure 2 by 3½ inches, and then paste the narrow ends to the sides of a small wooden or cardboard matchbox. Round hard candies form the wheels; paste them in place. Run a string through the front, knot it on the inside and fill the wagon with some candy surprises.

ENVELOPE GREETING

An unusual greeting card that stands up can be made from any used envelope that has a cellophane window. Cut around the window as shown, write your message on the inside under the cellophane and sign your name. Decorate the outside with a colorful design. This same stand-up card may be used as a place card simply by writing a name under the cellophane window.

BOWL OF FRUIT

Any little friend would be happy to receive this tiny bowl of fruit. The bowl is a metallic-paper candy cup with the top edges folded down. To make the fruit, take pieces of wax from a candle and knead it with shavings from old crayons, using the proper crayon color for each fruit. Now with your fingers mold the colored wax into apples, bananas, oranges and other fruit. The fruit stems are simply little pieces of string, stuck into the wax. They will look real enough to tempt anyone to take a bite.

PENCIL HOLDER

61319

Use an empty cellophane tape dispenser to make this handy pencil holder. Just pull out the sides of the dispenser as shown, then paint it all over with red nail polish. When the polish dries, slip the pencils through the holes. This gadget can also be used to hold paint brushes. It makes a nice gift for an artist friend.

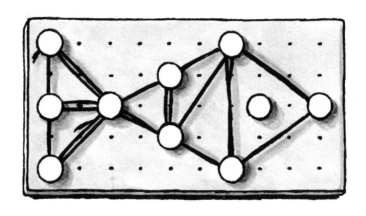

THUMBTACK FISH

Thumbtacks usually come on rectangles of thick cardboard which make fine bases for unusual designs. First press tacks into the holes to form the outline of an object, then wind string or wool around the tacks. Make the modernistic fish shown above, then try a few of your own designs such as dog, tree or house.

2. Holiday Gifts

FUZZY-WUZZY

Make a fuzzy-wuzzy for a sick friend or for an Easter gift. Cut an animal shape from construction paper. Glue cotton to the entire surface. When the glue dries, remove the excess cotton and cut away the fuzz that laps over the edges. Draw the face with pencil and glue a strip of paper to the back, as shown, to make animal stand up.

VALENTINE BASKET

This Valentine basket is made from red construction paper that measures 4½ by 9 inches. Fold the paper in half so you have a square. Cut the heart-shape top through the two thicknesses. Then tape the open side of the basket shut. Decorate with designs cut from a lace paper doily and attach string handles. Place a Valentine card or a small gift in the basket and give it to a friend.

HEART BOOKMARK

Here's how to make a heart bookmark for your Valentine. First, fold a 3½-inch square of red paper in half. Draw the half-heart pattern as shown, then cut it out through the two thicknesses. Cut a lining for the heart from plain white paper, making this the same shape but a bit wider than the red heart. Now paste both hearts together and paste a red or white ribbon to the back of the hearts.

SPRINGTIME BOUQUET

To make this bouquet, cut slits along straight narrow strips of crepe paper. Then paste the paper to the backs of cardboard milk-bottle tops, fanning it out as you go. Use green toothpicks for stems and run them into the side of the milk-tops. Tie the flowers together with ribbon and fasten the bouquet to a lapel with a straight pin. A single flower makes a nice boutonniere for a boy's lapel.

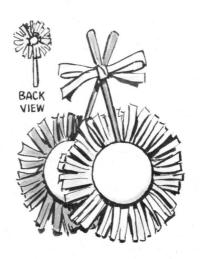

BACK VIEW

EASTER CHICK

This chick is just a decorated hard-boiled egg. Make the beak from a piece of colored cellophane tape. Cut it into a point and fasten the ends to the egg. The tail is colored ribbon that has been cut into strips as shown, then pasted in place. Draw the eyes with pencil, then balance the egg on a round candy base.

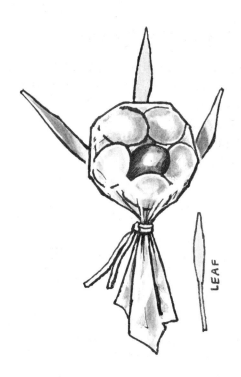

LEAF

JELLY-BEAN BOUQUET

Anyone would be happy to receive a colorful jelly-bean bouquet at Eastertime. To make it, cut a few narrow leaves from green construction paper by following the pattern. Then place about seven jelly beans in the center of a cellophane paper square, arrange the leaves and tie it up with string.

COTTON BUNNY

Make bunny's head and body by daubing a toothpick with paste, then winding absorbent cotton around it to make two balls joined at the neck. Cut ears, eyes, nose and mouth from colored paper and paste them in place. Stick the end of the toothpick into a chocolate Easter egg. It's a special treat!

BACK
VIEW

EASTER CARD

From a seed packet, catalog or magazine cut a flower picture. Then fold a piece of paper in half and paste the flower close to the fold. Cut around the outline of the picture, leaving a wide border on all sides. Punch two holes along the fold, run a colored string through, and tie a bow of ribbon. Now write your Easter message on the inside of the card.

WATERPROOF BASKET

Give this waterproof flower basket to someone you like on May Day. Make it from an empty waxed cardboard container, such as butter or cottage cheese comes in. Cut a narrow strip all around the top rolled rim to form the handles. (See sketch.) Then pull the handles up and tie them together with a ribbon. Decorate the basket by cutting a lace-paper doily in half and fastening the pieces to the sides with cellophane tape, covering up any name that might be on the basket.

MAY BASKET

A dainty May basket can be made from half of a paper doily. Bring the corners marked "X" together and roll into a cone shape. Tape the side in place. Then make a lining from a smaller half-circle of wax paper and drop that inside the cone. Now attach a long ribbon handle, fill the basket with flowers and hang the basket on a friend's door.

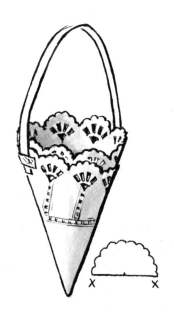

APPLE POT

Fall holiday time is a good time to have some apple pots ready to serve to your friends. To make one, cut off the top of an apple just below the stem, then scoop out the middle part to remove the seeds. Run three toothpicks through the bottom to form the base. Fill the middle with a mixture of jelly and nuts. An apple pot should be eaten the same day it is made.

APPLE STICK

Hallowe'en time is giving time, so have apple sticks ready to give to your friends. Cut two pieces of red construction paper into an apple shape, sew the sides together with yarn, leaving a small opening at the top. Write name, then insert a lollypop and close top with cellophane tape.

1   CUT

2

ENVELOPE TEPEE

Decorate the table at Thanksgiving (or any time) with envelope tepees. To make one, place a kitchen saucer over a corner of an envelope, trace around it and cut on this line. (See sketch 1.) Make the entrance by cutting along the dotted line of sketch 2. Draw Indian designs. Now open the envelope and pinch in the top corner until the tepee stands up.

YULE SEAL LOCKET

Show that you have made a gift to the Tuberculosis Association by wearing a Christmas seal locket or give one to a contributor. To make this locket, knead a piece of candle wax and flatten it to about 1/8 inch in thickness. Paste a seal to the wax and with scissors trim the wax edges, leaving a border. To the back of the locket paste another seal. Now run a string through a hole at the top.

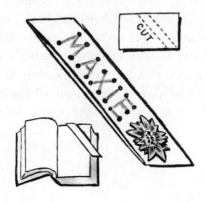

ENVELOPE BOOKMARK

A useful Christmas present that you can make for any member of your family is this bookmark. Cut a band *at an angle* across a sealed envelope. (See the small sketch.) Write the person's name with crayon or paint, then decorate the lower corner of the bookmark with a Christmas seal. Slip the corner of the book page through the opening in the bookmark and the decorated corner will stick out at the side.

HOLIDAY PLAQUE

Make a glistening holiday plaque from an empty tin container, the kind that herring or sardines come in. Remove the top of the can completely and wash the inside very carefully. Then make a hole at the top with a nail and a hammer. Now mix poster paint with soap powder and paint a picture on the bottom of the can. You can also paint over any printing on the sides of the can. Run a string through the hole and hang it on the Christmas tree or a wall.

CHRISTMAS ANGEL

From plain white paper cut a half-circle that measures 8 inches across. Paste the ends over each other, as in sketch 2. Cut a ¼-inch border from a paper muffin cup and slip it over the cone-shaped body. Then use the muffin cup center to make the head and tape it in place. Form the wings from the remaining piece of the muffin cup and tape it to the angel's back.

SNOWMAN HOLDER

This snowman makes a fine holder for a gift comb or handkerchief. First, cut the snowman from the paper padding that comes in candy boxes. Then outline it on plain white paper and cut another exactly the same shape. Sew the two pieces together with red yarn but leave the top open. Glue on colored paper facial features and buttons. Hang it from the Christmas tree.

3. Novelties to Use

SERPENTINE SNAKE

Make a serpentine snake centerpiece for your party table from an old nylon stocking and some apples. Drop an apple into the stocking and tie a knot. Repeat this until the stocking is filled, then sew up the stocking end and sew button eyes to the head.

Before the party is over be sure to give each guest "a piece of snake" to take home. This is an especially good table decoration for Hallowe'en.

NEW NOTE PAPER

Used greeting cards that have a double fold can be made into useful note paper by cutting away the insides at the fold (usually at the top). In this way the original message can be removed. Now the new inside of your cards may be used for notes or any greetings that you wish to write.

SALT-BOX BANK

Save your pennies, nickels and dimes in a bank made from an empty salt box, the kind that has a metal spout at the top. Cover the box with plain white paper. Then from an old magazine cut the letters that spell your name and paste them to the box. To make your deposits just lift the metal spout, drop your money in and press the spout down flat again.

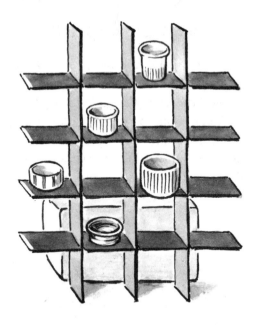

DISPLAY RACK

The cardboard webbing that is used in candy boxes to separate pieces of candy can easily be turned into a display rack. Simply stand it up on one end and rest it against a wall. If the webbing falls to one side, bend it over flat to the other side, so it will balance when you open it up again. Use the shelves to display a colorful collection of plastic and metal bottle caps or any tiny toys and knickknacks that you happen to have.

REFRESHMENT KIT

You will find this refreshment kit quite handy, especially when you entertain outdoors or go on a picnic. All you do is cover the cardboard "handy-pack" (the kind that bottled soda comes in) with fancy wrapping paper or patterned wallpaper. Then you can use the different compartments to hold napkins, straws, a jar of peanut butter and other items that you need.

HAIRPIN HANGER

Here is a good way to hang up one of your own drawings or a picture cut from a magazine without making a
hole in the paper. Fasten two gummed reinforcements to
the back of the picture at the top, then twist an ordinary
hairpin into a loop as shown. Run hairpin ends through
the reinforcements and hang the loop on a nail.

LEMON-SKIN BOWL

As you can see, this attractive bowl is made from half of a lemon. (When Mother uses lemon juice for cooking ask her to save the skin for you.) Remove all the pulp from the inside, then make the legs by breaking toothpicks in half and sticking them into the skin. Fill the bowl with raisins or tiny candies.

WATERING CAN

This useful pitcher that may be used to water your plants is made from an empty milk carton and some heavy twine. First, cut the top of the spout as shown in the illustration. Then with the twine tie two very tight bands around the carton. Now attach a twine handle to the bands.

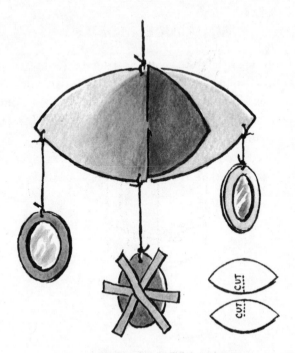

COLORED-PAPER MOBILE

A mobile is fun to make. Suspended from the ceiling, it will sway and turn in the slightest breeze, offering constant interest.

The mobile shown above is made by cutting construction paper into two fish shapes, 4½-inches long by 2½-inches wide. Slit each fish shape to its center (see small diagrams) and lock one into the other. Make the end circles by pasting colored cellophane between two circular bands of construction paper. Decorate both sides of the middle circle with construction paper of another color. Connect all parts with heavy thread.

MINIATURE MOBILE

Another mobile that is interesting to look at can be made from wire and tiny objects found around the house. Make the base from a bottle by filling it with sand, modeling clay or a heavy stone. Fasten wire to the base, then attach tiny objects to form a well-balanced design. Bells, beads, colored-paper designs and jelly beans may be used. A slight breeze will move the hanging mobile.

MILK-CAP CHICK

To make this cute little chick fasten two milk-bottle caps together with cellophane tape (see inset). Paste a red paper beak in place, then glue a thin layer of absorbent cotton to the milk caps. Run straight pin legs into the body and draw the eye with pencil. Use the chick to decorate a cake or a potted plant at Easter.

SILVERWARE HOLDER

From a paper napkin you can make a very useful silverware holder. Place the napkin with the unfolded edges at the top, then take the first top corner and fold it down to the bottom corner (see sketch 1). Fold the sides back along the dotted lines of sketch 2. Decorate with a sticker or a magazine picture and place the silverware in the pocket for a place setting.

PARTY PLACE MATS

Here is a place mat with loops that will hold a fork and a spoon for a very young party. It can be made from a construction paper sheet and a strip of paper a half-inch wide. Cut four slits at one side of the mat where the silver will go. Then from the back weave the narrow strip through. On the back, tape the strip end down, turn the mat over and pull up the strip to form loops. Write the name on the end piece. Make separate place mats for all of your little guests the next time you have a party.

SNACK APPLE

When your class goes to the zoo or when you play outdoors, a good way to take an apple along is to make a snack apple that can be worn around your neck. First, core the apple to remove the seeds. Then wind a 4-inch band of wax paper around one section of a string. Run this through the apple center and knot the ends of the string to form a loop which can be slipped over your head.

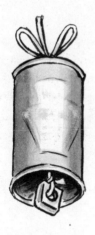

DINNER BELL

This bell is made from an empty juice or soup can, a metal nut from a nut-and-bolt combination and 10 inches of heavy string. First, punch a hole through the top of the can. Now attach the metal nut at one end of the string. Then run the other end of the string through the hole and knot it close to the hole. Tie a bow. You can paint over the printed label on the can or paste a design on the can itself to make a handsome dinner bell.

PICTURE STAND-UP

Many of the greeting cards you receive during the holiday season can easily be turned into third-dimensional pictures. Just cut around the sides and top of a pictured object. Then fold it up right along the bottom (uncut) line.

You can make a whole village to play with by cutting around buildings and clusters of trees. A stand-up candle or cuddly animal makes a nice place card.

JAR-TOP CANDLEHOLDER

All you need to make this type of candleholder are a metal jar top and a pipe cleaner. Twist the pipe cleaner around the jar top to form the handle as shown. Now place a tiny candle in the middle and secure it with a few drops of melted wax. A pair of candleholders will make attractive holiday decorations.

TOY UMBRELLA

To make a useful toy umbrella flatten a fluted-paper cookie cup along the edges. Then push a thumbtack through the center and into the top of a burned matchstick. Now whittle down the other end of the match and fit it into a macaroni-bend handle. By turning the umbrella upside down and filling it with candy you will have a nice party favor.

4. Novelties to Wear

PIRATE EARRING

Make a pirate earring from a rubber band and a piece of gold or silver paper 5 inches long by 1 inch wide. Fold the paper in half the long way, then in half again in the same direction. This will give you a long strip which you pass through the rubber band. Paste the ends of the paper together, and bend the strip into a circle. To wear this pirate earring, all you do is slip the rubber band over your ear.

PAPER BAG PARTY HAT

This party hat is made from a flat paper bag. With the bottom of the bag forming the back of the hat, cut the bag square as shown. Then fold the corners up. Run a string through each side just above the fold and knot each end. Tape the ends in place and decorate the turned-up corners with crayon.

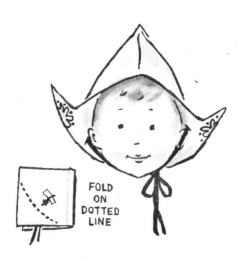

FOLD
ON
DOTTED
LINE

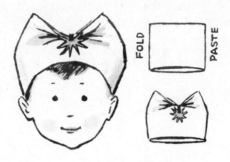

WRAPPING PAPER HAT

Another kind of party hat can be made from a piece of leftover tissue paper or fancy wrapping paper 22 inches long by 9 inches wide. Fold the paper in half (to 11 x 9) and paste the ends together. Now gather the hat at the top center with a strip of colored tape. A paper ornament may be attached to the tape as shown in the illustration.

FRIENDSHIP BRACELET

To make this bracelet, cover milk-bottle tops or cardboard circles with silver paper. Make a hole at the top of each circle. Then paint the initials of friends and relatives on them with red nail polish. Run a colored string through the holes and tie the string into a bow. You can always add more silver charms to your friendship bracelet or replace the ones you started with.

DRESS-UP BRAIDS

An attractive pair of "fake" braids can be made out
of six old nylon stockings, three for each braid. First, attach three of the stockings by sewing the tops together.
Now make a braid out of these and secure the end with a
rubber band. Do this again with the other three stockings
for the second braid. Trim the braids with ribbon bows,
bells, nuts and any small trinkets you might have. Fasten
the braids to your head with bobby pins.

CROWN OF LAUREL

A good homemade costume is that of an ancient Greek philosopher. A crown of laurel, sandals and an old sheet draped over your shoulders and belted at the waist are all you need. The crown of laurel is made from a band of wrapping paper 1½ inches wide and long enough to fit around your head. Cut leaves from construction paper and paste them to the band.

SANDALS

The soles of these Grecian sandals are cardboard. Place your right foot on the cardboard and trace around it. Cut it out now and cut another one the same way for your left foot. Now tear streamers of cotton material, making them about ½-inch wide, 12 to 18 inches long. Run one streamer through the four holes near the toes, as shown. Run another streamer through two holes at the heel and wind it around your leg.

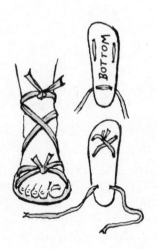

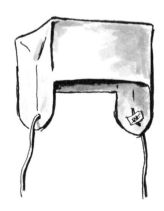

FOOTBALL HELMET

Make a football helmet from a flat-bottomed paper bag that is large enough to fit over your head. Cut the bag as shown. Run string through the ear pieces, knot the string ends, then tape the knots to the bag on the inside. Wear the helmet while watching games on television.

NURSE'S CAP

Shelf paper or white wrapping paper that measures 20 by 13 inches may be used to make this nurse's cap. Cut out the shaded portion shown on the diagram. Fold the narrow (3″) band at the bottom in half the long way. Then bring the ends of this strip to the back of the center section and pin them in place. You now have a cap. Bobby pins can hold it in place.

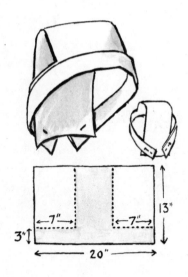

FALSE MUSTACHE

This realistic mustache that may be worn on Hallowe'en or any time is made from a piece of heavy twine about 4½ inches long. Unravel the twine ends, then fasten the strands tightly together in the center with cellophane tape. Allow one end of the tape to extend so it can be taped to your upper lip.

LOONY GLASSES

To make these glasses all you will need are an empty bathroom-tissue roll and some pipe cleaners. Make the false nose by cutting the top of the bathroom-tissue roll as shown in the small sketch. Now punch holes on both sides of the cut-out V at the top of the nose, insert pipe cleaner "lenses" with attached earpieces.

TOY EYEGLASSES

To make these eyeglasses you just need two pipe cleaners and colored tape. First twist one end of the pipe cleaners into a circle, as shown, then bend the earpieces into shape. Now make the colored frames by winding small strips of tape around the pipe cleaners. Fasten them together with a nosepiece made from another strip of tape.

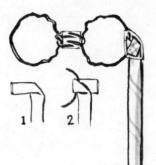

TOY LORGNETTES

Treat yourself to a pair of lorgnettes. First bend two small wire hairpins into circular eyepiece shapes. Form the nosepiece by winding cellophane tape around the hairpin ends. Attach a soda straw to the wire frame by folding the straw top over (sketch 1), then bending the straw around wire (sketch 2). Now fold the straw down again and fasten in place with cellophane tape.

COLORED GLASSES

To make the colored glasses sketched here, cut away the centers of two milk-bottle caps. Punch holes in both sides of the caps, attach pipe cleaner earpieces, then use half of a pipe cleaner for the nosepiece. Removable "lenses" are made from circles of colored cellophane, taped in place. Use yellow or pink lenses for a cheery outlook, and blue or green for sunglasses.

CANDY EARRINGS

Candy motto hearts that are so popular around Valentine's Day may be used to make a pair of earrings. Use three hearts for each earring. Fasten them together on a strip of cellophane tape, then fold the tape over a rubber band. On Valentine's Day wear these candy earrings by fitting the rubber bands over your ears and letting the candy hearts dangle.

MILK-CAP WATCH

The tinfoil cap which comes on a small bottle that holds a glassful of milk may be used to make this toy wrist watch. Bend the sides down flat to form the watch frame, then draw the watch face with pencil or ink. With cellophane tape attach a rubber band to the back of the watch.

TOY POCKET WATCH

This toy pocket watch and chain are made by placing the circular end of a curtain pull on a piece of paper and tracing around the outside as well as the inside of it. Cut along the outer circle, draw a clock face within the inner circle and now paste it to the back. Slip a metal paper clip through the string end.

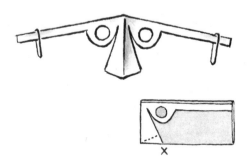

NOSE GOGGLES

These nose goggles can be made from an ordinary business envelope. Cut away the shaded areas of the envelope, as shown. Then push up the area marked X (which will be your nose tip) and fold along the dotted line. Slip a rubber band over each side piece, place the side pieces over your ears, and fit the rubber bands over your ears to hold nose goggles in place.

PAPER BAG MOCCASINS

Two flat-bottomed paper bags will make a pair of moccasins that can be worn with a dress-up costume or when you want to protect your shoes from the muddy outdoors after a rain. With your shoes on, slip your feet into the bags. Ribbon or string tied just above the ankles will hold the moccasins in place. If the weather is threatening and you must go somewhere, it is a good idea to take along two bags and string to protect your shoes.

SHERLOCK HOLMES CAP

All you need to be a detective are a Sherlock Holmes cap and a magnifying glass. Make the cap from a flat-bottomed paper bag. Cut the bag by following the dotted lines of the diagram. Then tape up the side flaps and turn up the front and back visors. The four corners at the top may be taped down with cellophane tape.

MAGNIFYING GLASS AND FINGERPRINTS

You can make this magnifying glass from a box that has a cellophane "window." First draw the outline of the magnifying glass, then cut it out. A good way to study fingerprints is to run your fingers over a moist cake of soap. Then press your fingertips down on a small mirror. Look at them through your magnifying glass.

NOISEMAKER

A dandy noisemaker can be made from an empty frozen-juice can. Be sure the top has been cleanly removed. Place one end of the can on a piece of cardboard and trace around it. Then cut out the circle. Put a few marbles or buttons in the can and close up the open end with the cardboard circle.

Decorate the noisemaker with bands of red nail polish —or paint the can with enamel. After the polish or enamel is dry, glue a couple of pictures to the can.

5. Dolls to Make

STUFFED CAT

This washable stuffed toy is made from a plastic bag that fresh vegetables come in. First, make the head by crumpling tissue paper into a ball and placing it in the bag. Tie a ribbon at the neck and then stuff the body with a larger tissue paper ball. Tie again with ribbon. Now twist the open end into a pointed tail and secure it with tape. Paint the facial features with enamel.

STOCKING DOLL

Cut an old nylon stocking across the sole, as shown, saving the two parts. Cut the stocking leg into four equal pieces. To make the head, stuff the tip of the toe with one stocking piece. Twist a pipe cleaner around the neck, and this will also form the arms. Stuff the doll's body with the remaining pieces. Place a pipe cleaner across the opening and sew it up. Bend the pipe cleaner as shown in the sketch to make the legs and feet. Make the facial features with stitches of thread.

TOY GUARDSMAN

This toy guardsman is made from a hard-boiled egg head, a paper-cup hat with a twine cockade and a cardboard tube body. One 8-inch length of twine forms both arms. Cut slots at the top of the tube for the arms to fit through. (See inset.) Wind tape at the wrists, then tape the arms to the sides. Paint on the facial features, buttons and belt.

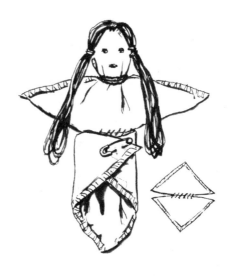

INDIAN BABY

This cuddly Indian baby is made from two shoulder pads sewn together, as shown. Wind a rubber band around the top corner of the upper pad to make the head. For hair, use 8-inch lengths of black yarn, stitching them to the head at the part and at the sides. Sew the facial features with thread. Fold over the side ends of the lower pad and fasten them in place with a safety pin.

SOCK PUPPET

Cut the top of an old sock into three sections (along the dotted lines) and plait them into a braid. Tie the ends with string and attach a bell. Now cut away the tip of the toe. Stuff the stocking to fill the half towards the heel, forming the head of the doll. Then wind a rubber band at the neck. Sew on button eyes and paint a mouth. Now you can put your hand inside the stocking with your middle finger up into the head and make the puppet act.

WALNUT SHELL CRADLE

Make this little toy cradle for a doll from half of a walnut shell. Cut two pieces of string the same size, then fasten them to the bottom of the shell with cellophane tape and knot the string ends together. Use absorbent cotton for a pillow and make a doll from a burnt paper matchstick or a tiny cut-out.

TAP-DANCING PUPPET

To make this puppet, run a 10-inch length of twine through a two-hole button (see sketch). Slip a small plastic cap or cork into the twine loop to form the head. Then run the twine through an empty spool and another button below it. Pull the twine tight and tie a knot. After you've added button "feet," paint the face on one side of the plastic cap or cork. Attach a 13-inch string to the top string and the puppet is now ready for action.

CARDBOARD DOLL

A lovable paper doll can be made from the light-weight cardboard of a cereal box and dressed in clothes made from scraps of material. First, draw a 5-inch square on the cardboard. Within the square draw the body of the doll and then above the square draw the doll's head and neck (see small sketch). Make a pencil line across the legs 1 inch up from the bottom. Now cut out the doll, draw facial features and hair. Bend up its feet on the pencil line.

SUN SUIT AND HAT

To make this sun suit for the cardboard doll, cut any fabric material twice as long as the width. Sew the raw edges under. Then make the halter from a strip of embroidery edging and sew it in place, as shown. Attach string to the sides of the suit. Now place the embroidery loop over the doll's head, pull the material under and to the back. Tie the strings together.

The hat is made from a circle of fabric material with a small slit cut down the center (see small inset).

PERSONALIZED SHOPPING BAG

Your doll will be proud to carry this shopping bag. It is 1½ inches wide; cut it from the corner of an ordinary flat paper bag. Then fold over the open side and paste it down. Tape string handles to the top and decorate with a cut-out initial. The shopping bag may be filled with small pictures of canned food and bottled beverages cut from old magazines.

DOLL'S RAINCOAT

From a paper bag you can make this attractive hooded raincoat for your doll. Using the corner at the bag top to form the hood, cut away the shaded areas of the small sketch, then slit the side of the bag as marked. Place the hood on the doll's head, wrap the raincoat around the doll and use cellophane tape as a side fastener, as shown. Now, when you want to take your doll along with you in the spring, she will be all prepared for April showers.

FRONT

BACK

TOP

DOLL'S WHIRLING SKIRT

An attractive skirt can be made from a circle of cotton print or plaid. (You may trace the circle around a dinner plate.) Cut a small circle in the center of the material large enough to fit the doll's waist, then make a slit to go in the back. (See small sketch.) Turn in all raw edges and stitch. Sew a long ribbon that ties in the back to the waist. Trim with rickrack.

PARTY BLOUSE

Curtain material or any sheer material can be used to make this blouse. The back and front are just two squares of material. Stitch all raw edges to the wrong side, then sew the squares together at the top. (See second small sketch.) Allow enough room in the center for the head to go through. The open sides of the blouse are lapped over each other and are tucked into the skirt.

SHOES FOR DOLLY

Treat your doll to a pair of open-toe summertime shoes made from paper candy cups. First, press one side of the candy cup down flat to make the sole of the shoe. Now fit the shoe on to the doll. Make the tie front by running string through the sides with a large embroidery needle. Tie the shoestring of each shoe into a bow.

DOLL'S SAFETY CHAIR

Make a doll's safety chair from a cardboard box, the kind that ink comes in. Use an empty milk carton for a large-sized doll. Cut the box as shown in small sketch, then make the tray by folding down the front along the dotted line. Cut out a section for the doll's legs to come through. Decorate with a crayon design.

6. Toys to Make

ZOO CAGE

Make a zoo cage from some string and an empty facial tissue box that has an oval-shaped opening. Punch holes along the sides of the opening, as shown. Knot the string at one end and lace it through the holes.

If you want, you can use a shoe box. Cut a hole in the lid, make the bars the same way and tape the lid to the box.

ANIMAL CUT-OUTS

Fill a zoo cage with animal pictures found in old magazines or with animal drawings. Cut closely along the outline of the animal, but do not cut around the legs; instead, cut the paper straight across the bottom. Now fold a strip of plain white paper in half and paste one side to the back of the cut-out (see small sketch). The animal will stand up and look alive.

TUBE TOM-TOM

This tom-tom is made from a cardboard tube. Cover both ends of the tube with tissue paper circles and use rubber bands to hold the paper securely in place. Now run string or colored wool under the rubber bands to form the tension cords. Beat the top of the drum with your fingertips. You might get several of your friends to make drums of their own. Then you can have fun by playing "Indians" and sending messages to one another.

ISOLATION BOOTH

A toy isolation booth, like the ones that contestants go into on television quiz programs, can be made from an empty cardboard milk carton. First draw the outline of the windows on all four sides of the carton with pencil. Now cut cardboard along the pencil lines. To make the door, cut one of the window sides down to the base and also cut along the base as shown.

MATCHBOX BOAT

A toy speedboat that will really float in water can be made from a small, sliding-drawer matchbox. First cut along the sides of the matchbox cover. Fold the top as shown and tape it in place. Draw a steering wheel and speedometer on the dashboard (the raised cover). Then run a knotted string through the front of the boat and you can pull it through your bathtub or pond.

PAPER VILLAGE

Used (or new) envelopes can quickly be turned into buildings by first cutting a roof shape at the top, then slitting the sides 1½ inches up from the bottom. Fold up the bottoms to form the base and paste extra paper across the underside of the base for better balance. Draw the front of the buildings with crayon or pencil on the blank backs of the envelopes. A complete paper village can be made by using different kinds of envelopes and by cutting the rooftops into a variety of shapes.

PUPPET STAGE

An empty tissue box makes a dandy puppet stage. Cut the box opening as shown. If you wish, removable scenery may be painted on construction paper and taped to the back of the stage. Punch a hole at the top and run the puppet string through. Tie the string end to a button and the other end to your puppet. (Puppet-making directions are on page 95.) Now move the string to make puppet dance, sit or lie down.

MILK-CARTON TRUCK

This truck is made from an empty milk carton. First, cut away the shaded areas as shown in the bottom sketch, then slit the bottom along the dotted line. Press the front piece in to form the dashboard. Now press the extended top down to form the back of the driver's section. (It can be taped into place.) Fasten cardboard circle wheels to the truck with thumbtacks.

TOY TRAINS

These toy trains are made from empty little cardboard candy boxes. Pull the flaps out along one side, then cover the boxes with paper and use rubber cement to hold it in place. Draw the sides of the train with crayon or ink. Glue the button wheels in place. Attach the trains by fastening the flaps together with cellophane tape.

BIRD'S NEST AND TREE

Wet half of a cleansing tissue and mold it into the shape of a nest. Squeeze out as much water as possible and allow nest to dry overnight. Make birds by painting dried orange seeds with water colors. Tape the nest to a twig and place the twig in the ground.

A toy village may be built around this scene. Or you can make a "forest" with nests.

BOTTLE-CAP BUG

The head of this bug is made from a metal screw-on cap and the body is made from soda-bottle caps. Fold strips of colored tape in half to form the feelers, then tape them to the head. Fasten the head to the body caps with more tape. Place the bug on a flat surface, then move the head to make the body wiggle.

SPOON MOUSE

Twist a pipe cleaner around a wooden spoon and bend the ends under, as shown. Draw the face with pencil. Then from paper cut out ears and tape them to the back. When you are entertaining stick the mouse into a square of cheese or hang it over the rim of a drinking glass. It is sure to get a laugh from your friends.

TOY ELEVATOR

Use the long narrow box that tooth paste comes in to make this toy elevator. First, cut away the front of the box except for ¾ of an inch at the bottom (see sketch 1). Now cut away the top of the box (on the dotted line) one inch from the top. Fit the flap over the side tabs and tape it down to the inside (sketch 2) to form the elevator base.

"Passengers" can be cut from newspaper comics. A straight pin taped to their backs and stuck into the elevator base will enable them to stand. Draw floor levels as shown, then fit the elevator into the shaft and the passengers are ready to ride.

FOLD ALONG
DOTTED LINE

TOY SAILBOAT

Waxed cardboard from an empty milk carton can be used to make a sailboat that will really float. First cut the cardboard 1¾ inches wide and 4 inches long. Cut the bow shape at one end, then slit the center for the sail to fit in. Make the sail from a triangle of the waxed cardboard and fold the bottom edge under (see small sketch). Now fit the sail into the slit and decorate the boat with a crayon border.

7. Novelties to Play With

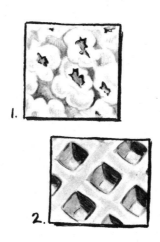

1.

2.

PUZZLE PICTURES

A very satisfactory puzzle can be made by cutting a one-inch square from colored food pictures from old magazines and pasting them to a sheet of paper. Number the squares and identify them on the backs. Now see how many pictures your friends and family can identify correctly. Those in the accompanying illustration are cut from pictures of popcorn and waffles.

TUBE WRITING

You can write on cardboard in a style that is like the fancy writing on birthday cakes. Cut away the bottom (not the cap) end of an empty tooth paste tube and with a pencil separate the tube sides. Wash the tube out. Mix a paste of flour and water until it is like cream. Add ink or dye to the paste. Now screw the cap in place on the tube and spoon the mixture into the tube. To write, remove the cap and squeeze out the paste.

STAMP JIGSAW

To make this jigsaw you will need nine cancelled postage stamps. By using different kinds and colors of stamps you can work out an interesting design. Arrange the stamps in rows of three, paste them to a piece of paper, then cut away the paper edges. Now on this stamp arrangement draw an X, make a circle in the middle and draw a line from the center of each side to the circle. Cut along these lines. Your jigsaw pieces will have similar shapes but will not be so easy for your friends to put together.

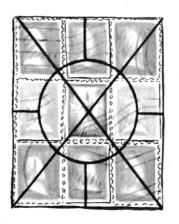

JIGSAW UTILITY BAG

The cellophane wrapping that has been slipped off of a box or a cellophane vegetable bag can be used to keep the pieces of your jigsaw together. Tying up the bag with a piece of colored string will make it into an attractive gift for a friend. This small cellophane bag can also be used to hold stamps or coins you collect or to display insects.

JELLY-BEAN BASKET

Slip the cellophane wrapping very carefully off of a cigarette pack and use it to make this attractive basket. Put some jelly beans into this little cellophane bag, then make the handle by folding a strip of colored tape or paper in half, lengthwise. Attach the handle and fasten the top sides together, as shown, with colored cellophane tape.

PUDDLE PAINTING

Puddle painting is a way of making unusual and colorful designs. With water colors and a thick brush drop puddles of paint on a sheet of paper that has a smooth surface. Blow the paint into puddles or tilt the paper to control the direction of your designs. The results can be most interesting.

TELEVISION SHOW

You can produce your own television shows. All you do is cut away one end of a used envelope and cut a rectangular opening to form the screen. Draw faces on your fingertips with ink. Then place your finger "actors" inside the envelope. Write program titles and advertise your sponsors' products on cards that may be slipped up through the envelope.

SOAP PAINTING

The thin sliver that is left over from a used cake of soap can be the base for a very attractive picture. (White soap is especially suitable.) Be sure the soap is dry. Now paint your pictures with water colors. Any time that you want to change your picture, wash away the surface paint and begin all over again.

JIGSAW PUZZLE

You can make an excellent jigsaw puzzle by using the entire front of an empty cardboard box, the kind that crackers, soap powders or cereals come in. After you have cut the front away from the rest of the box, divide the oblong shape into smaller sections by tracing around a dinner plate. Then cut along these lines. You'll get some queer-looking shapes.

FROSTY FINGER PAINTING

Mix a heaping teaspoon of flour with enough water to form a paste-like cream. Tape the corners of a dark or brightly-colored sheet of construction paper to a cardboard backing. Now use your fingers to "paint" with the flour mixture. The white, frosted effect is most unusual.

INDEX